Having Done All, Stand

i

Having Done All, Stand

BRYAN MATTHEWS

Cover Design by Carolynn Collins

Interior Design by Holly Murray

Edited by Holly Murray

iv

Contents

A Note to the Reader

I want to thank you for the opportunity of sharing some experiences together as you explore the pages before you! One of the greatest joys in my life is having the chance to help someone reach their life's goals and be able to see their dreams become a reality.

This book was not written from the perspective that I have arrived, and you can learn from me. Instead, it was written from the place that I have learned some hard lessons from mistakes I have made as well as having some successes along the way. If I can help you to avoid making the mistakes that I made, then you will be better able to run your race and reach your full potential.

Finally, a quick reminder. Don't be so focused on your destination, that you forget to enjoy the journey!

God Bless,
Bryan Matthews

Chapter 1
Is Your Life Dry?

Have you ever felt as though your life was an ongoing drought? Have you been waiting on a promise that you feel God has given you, but nothing is happening? Have you been standing and waiting on a prophetic word to come to pass, but Heaven seems quiet and you see no changes? If you have ever felt like that or are in a season of waiting even now, you are not alone!

In 1 Kings, we find that Israel had been in a drought for several years. Finally, a word came through the prophet Elijah that the drought was about to be broken. 1 Kings 18:41-45 reads:

> Then Elijah said to Ahab, "Go up, eat and drink; for there is the sound of abundance of rain." So Ahab went up to eat and drink. And Elijah went up to the top of Carmel; then he bowed down on the ground, and put his face between his knees, and said to his servant, "Go up now, look toward the sea." So he went up and looked, and said, "There is nothing." And seven times he said, "Go again." Then it came to pass the seventh time, that he said, "There is a cloud, as small as a man's hand, rising out of the sea!" So he said, "Go up, say to Ahab, 'Prepare your chariot, and go down before the rain stops you.'" Now it happened in the meantime that the sky became black with clouds and

wind, and there was a heavy rain. So Ahab rode away and went to Jezreel. (NKJV)

If your life feels dry or you are in a season of waiting, God wants to end the drought in your life. He is ready to pour out an abundance, not merely a sprinkle! But just because we have a word from the Lord does not mean that the word will automatically come to pass. There may be some things on *our* side of the equation that we need to do so that God can release His blessings on us.

In verse 42, Elijah went to the top of Mt. Carmel and got into a position of prayer. He knew he must birth his prophetic word from God with prayer. Only then did he tell his servant to go and look for rain. His servant went to look and returned with the report that he saw no change.

Seeing no changes in the natural does not alter God's original word. We must keep looking. Even though *we* see no change, God's Word does not change. Take your promise to God in prayer. Don't look at your current circumstances but keep looking for your promise to come!

When you can't cite a change in current circumstances, consider the certainty and consistency of God's Word.

Elijah sent his servant back to look again. He came the second time to report that he saw nothing different. And just like Elijah's servant, we sometimes must go look again! We cannot be moved by circumstances. We cannot be moved by bad news, emotion, or feelings. We must stand on what God has said. You have the Word of God and you have His promise, but have you quit looking? Have you quit expecting good things to happen?

When we stop expecting blessings to come our way, and our life feels dry, our faith is not where it needs to be. We cannot please God without faith. Hebrews 11:6a reads, "But without faith it is impossible to please Him" (NKJV). God cannot move in a realm where there is no faith. Faith is like fertilizer on seed. Go look again! Keep your expectation set on the Word of God, because God is able.

God cannot move in a realm where there is no faith.

So many times, we think that if it is God's will, then whatever we are believing for will come to pass. Will it? We know that it is God's will for all people to be saved, but all are not. God has done His part, and that's all He will do. He sent Jesus. He has given us the door, but it is our choice to walk through the door or not. He has shown us the path, but it is our decision to walk on it. Is your life dry? You have the choice to do something about that.

Chapter 2
What is Your Promise?

You may tell me that you have never received a prophetic word, but I tell you that you have at your disposal an entire Book full of promises for life, health, peace of mind, and prosperity in all you do—all located in the Word of God. We have many promises from God and obviously, they are all His will since He recorded them in the Bible. He let us know we could have them all. Psalm 84:34 says, "No, I will not break my covenant; I will not take back one word of what I said" (TLB). In 2 Corinthians 1:19b, Paul, referring to Jesus, wrote, "He isn't one to say yes when He means no" (TLB). The next verse continues, saying, "He carries out and fulfills all of God's promises, no matter how many of them there are; and we have told everyone how faithful He is, giving glory to His name" (TLB). God's promises are for us. What promise are you believing God for? Will it just automatically come to pass?

The Word tells us that we do not have to stand in our own strength, ability, or wisdom alone. Ephesians 6:10-13 admonishes us to put on the whole armor of God. It reads:

> Finally, my brethren, be strong in the Lord and in the power of His might. Put on the whole armor of God, that you may be able to stand against the wiles of the devil. For we do not wrestle against flesh and blood, but against principalities, against powers, against the rulers of the darkness of this age, against spiritual hosts

of wickedness in the heavenly places. Therefore take
up the whole armor of God, that you may be able to
withstand in the evil day, and having done all, to stand.
(NKJV)

We do not have to try and stand in our own righteousness, but
rather stand in Him and in the power of *His* might! In the
midnight hour, when the devil comes to say we don't deserve
a promise because of our past or something we may have
done, we won't stand in our own righteousness. We can point
him to the blood of Jesus that has washed us clean. We can
stand as a new creature—on His Word, on His blood, and on
His righteousness! Hallelujah!

God says to put on the whole armor. Don't leave
anything out. Don't leave any part off. If He recorded every
piece, then we need to use every piece. Each one is recorded
for a purpose.

When we stand against the "wiles" of the enemy, we
are standing against his schemes, plans, purposes, and agenda.
We do not wrestle against flesh and blood. Our problem is not
with the boss. In the morning before church, our problem isn't
our husband, our wife, or our kids. Our problem is the devil
trying to keep us out of the Word or from hearing the Word.

The enemy is trying to get your eyes off your true
purpose. He wants you to be preoccupied so that you will not
receive your promise or the Word of God. It seems he always
tries to attack on Saturday nights or Sunday mornings,
desiring to get you off on the wrong foot, interrupting your
sleep, or trying to keep you out of church completely.

Scripture says that we wrestle not against flesh and blood (Ephesians 6:12a, KJV), but we do wrestle. Make no mistake about it. We have a real enemy whose only purpose, Scripture tells us, is to steal, kill, and destroy (John 10:10, NKJV). There really is a devil who will not just lay back and let us enjoy all God's blessings and promises without putting up a fight.

We must never be frightened of him, but always remember the verse that reads, "He who is in you is greater than he who is in the world" (1 John 4:4, NKJV). The Greater One is within us, and we can choose to stand in the power of His might. We should never try to deal with the devil without the power of God's might working in us.

Ephesians 6:13 says, ". . . having done all" (NKJV). Have we done all? Did we go and look for the rain seven times as Elijah's servant did, or did we stop at six? Have we done absolutely everything He told us to do? Did He say seven and we chose to stop at five? Have we done what we were supposed to do? We have the promise, but have we waged warfare with the Word? We have the promise, we may have it pictured in our mind, but have we pressed toward the mark?

We have the promise, but have we waged warfare with the Word?

Maybe you are one who believes that your word from God will just come to pass automatically. Could there be something that you need to do? What is your promise and what has God told you to do about it? When God told Elijah that rain was coming, there was some work on Elijah's part to birth that prophetic word.

Chapter 3
Who or What is Your God?

In 2 Kings, we find Israel in another situation. It seems like Israel was always in a situation. It may seem to you that *you* are always in a situation! 2 Kings 3:6-18 reads:

> So King Joram marched out from Samaria at that time and mobilized all Israel. Then he sent a message to King Jehoshaphat of Judah: "The king of Moab has rebelled against me. Will you go with me to fight against Moab?"
>
> Jehoshaphat said, "I will go. I am as you are, my people as your people, my horses as your horses."
>
> Then he asked, "Which route should we take?"
>
> Joram replied, "The route of the Wilderness of Edom."
>
> So the king of Israel, the king of Judah, and the king of Edom set out. After they had traveled their indirect route for seven days, they had no water for the army or their animals.
>
> Then the king of Israel said, "Oh no, the Lord has summoned three kings, only to hand them over to Moab."
>
> But Jehoshaphat said, "Isn't there a prophet of the Lord here? Let's inquire of Yahweh (Jehovah) through him."
>
> One of the servants of the king of Israel answered, "Elisha son of Shaphat, who used to pour water on Elijah's hands, is here."

Jehoshaphat affirmed, "The Lord's words are with
him." So the king of Israel and Jehoshaphat and the
king of Edom went to him.
However, Elisha said to King Joram of Israel, "We
have nothing in common. Go to the prophets of your
father and your mother!"
But the king of Israel replied, "No, because it is the
Lord who has summoned these three kings to hand
them over to Moab."
Elisha responded, "As the Lord of Hosts lives, I stand
before Him. If I did not have respect for King
Jehoshaphat of Judah, I would not look at you; I
wouldn't take notice of you. Now, bring me a
musician."
While the musician played, the Lord's hand came on
Elisha. Then he said, "This is what the Lord says: 'Dig
ditch after ditch in this wadi [valley].' For the Lord
says, 'You will not see wind or rain, but the wadi will
be filled with water, and you will drink—you and your
cattle and your animals.' This is easy in the Lord's
sight. He will also hand Moab over to you. (HCSB)

We see here that a great army of Moab had come out
against the children of Israel. King Jehoram had asked King
Jehoshaphat to partner with him against the enemy, to which
King Jehoshaphat had agreed. After seven days they find
themselves in a situation of having no provisions. It is
impossible to move an army without water.

The king of Israel was not really a godly king. His
faith was only in what he could see, and he began to say that

God had brought them together to deliver them into the hands of the enemy. King Jehoshaphat of Judah refused to agree with that thinking. He said, "Is there no prophet of the Lord with us? If there is, we can ask the Lord what to do through him" (2 Kings 3:11, NLT). Remember that they did not have the privilege of the Holy Spirit to lead and guide them as we have under the new covenant. Thank God that we have a direct line to Heaven to know what to do in any situation!

When the kings called Elisha in, Elisha looked at the three kings and said to the ungodly King Jehoram of Israel, "What have I to do with you?" (2 Kings 3:13, NKJV). Another translation of the same verse records it this way, "We have nothing in common" (HCSB). Elisha questioned why King Jehoram of Israel didn't go to the gods he'd been praying to and serving to see if they would answer him now (2 Kings 3:13). These were harsh questions!

We must be cautious if we are not choosing to serve God, but then begin calling on Him just when we need help. If you are in the clubs on Saturday night and coming to church on Sunday to find help for problems you face, why not call the bartender for your answer? Who or what is your god? Why not see if that bottle can answer your problem? Why not see if that needle can get you out of the mess you are in? Maybe that relationship you're in that isn't of God can get you out of your mess? Go talk to the god that you have been serving! This makes it hit a little closer to home, doesn't it?

In 2 Kings 3:14, Elisha, directing his conversation to King Jehoram, the king of Israel, says, "As the Lord of Hosts lives, before whom I stand, surely, were it not for my regard for Jehoshaphat the king of Judah, I would not look at you nor see you" (MEV). King Jehoram had not made it a habit to honor the Lord. Elisha implied that it was only because of King Jehoram's association with King Jehoshaphat that he would go to God to inquire what to do at all. Those were strong words that Elisha used, but the company you choose to keep is very important. It matters who you hang out with and God is concerned with whom you associate. Thank God for grace. Thank God that we have a new covenant, one of mercy; but we still don't need to push it to the limit.

Choose carefully the company you keep – it matters.

Elisha instructs them to make the valley full of ditches. 2 Kings 3:16 (HCSB) reads, "This is what the Lord says: 'Dig ditch after ditch in this wadi [valley].'" This made no sense to the kings. They needed water, not ditches. But it is important to know who your God is. Many times, the instructions of God make no sense to our natural thinking, but it is not up to us to figure out the reasons behind the command. It is up to us to obey.

Why do we think we must have the answer before we do what He says to do? It is as if we think He needs to explain Himself to us. We should not ask questions like, "Lord, why must I forgive before this will happen?" when He has commanded us to forgive. It is not our place to ask why about everything. Rather, it is our place to do what He says. He is God.

In your situation, have you done all that you should? .
Have you done what God has told you to do, or have you done
only what you thought was necessary? Sometimes, in my life,
I do what I want to do, thinking it should be enough.
Obedience is not about what I think or feel.

It is not up to me to set the standards and then ask God
to back them. I may think looking back four times is enough,
so why should I go back and look seven times? It shouldn't
matter to me if He says look one thousand times! My
responsibility is to do exactly what He says. He is my God. If
He says to go back and look one thousand times, then I should
not question the thousand—I must *do* the thousand. Only then,
having done my all, am I able to stand. Standing represents
resting in Him. I can only rest in Him when I have done all He
has required me to do.

Standing represents resting in Him.

The command from the Lord spoken by Elisha was to
dig ditches. If God speaks to you to dig ditches, don't respond
with, "But God, I don't understand." It doesn't matter! If He is
your God, dig the ditches!

Have you stopped digging? Maybe you have your
word from God, but you've stopped pressing, looking, or
following through with His command. It's time to get your
shovel out. It's time to begin fully doing what God has
instructed you to do.

Chapter 4
Never Give Up

Following God's Word completely is important. You should never give up on a word from the Lord or compromise on what you've been instructed to do. 2 Kings 4 tells of a woman who, when her husband died, was left with nothing except a debt and no way to pay it. The creditor was coming to take her two sons away as slaves as payment for the loan. The widow knew the debt must be paid but went to Elisha for help.

The prophet Elisha asked her what she had in her house. She told him that all she had was a pot of oil. Sometimes, especially when we think what we have is not enough, we are not willing to give up that which we *do* have. We fail to realize that God is not trying to take something from us, but He must have a seed to multiply back to us. He cannot multiply nothing—zero multiplied by any number is still zero.

God wants to multiply what we have back to us.

Elisha told the widow, "Go, borrow vessels from everywhere, from all your neighbors—empty vessels; do not gather just a few" (2 Kings 4:3, NKJV). How many vessels did she need to get? All that she could! The prophet told her that when she gathered the vessels, she should pour oil from her pot into all the vessels that they had collected, and then "set aside the full ones" (2 Kings 4:4, NKJV). He is telling her exactly what to do to multiply what she already has.

Verse 5 says "So she left him and shut the door behind her and her sons, and they kept bringing vessels to her, and she kept pouring" (2 Kings 4:5, MEV). Where is your faith? Elisha told the widow not to borrow a few—in other words, borrow many! Her part was for her and her sons to collect as many vessels as they could, and they didn't give up. I would have sent those boys everywhere!

The widow began to pour the oil into the borrowed vessels. Scripture says, "When the vessels were full, she said to her son, 'Bring me another vessel.' But he said to her, 'There is not another vessel.' And the oil ceased" (2 Kings 4:6, MEV). What a miracle! She didn't give up. She did all she had been told to do. She fully obeyed the word of the Lord given by the prophet and saw amazing results. When she told the prophet Elisha what had happened, he told her, "Go, sell the oil and pay your debt; and you and your sons live on the rest" (2 Kings 4:7, NKJV).

Don't give up. Fully obey the word of the Lord.

The widow had done *all* she'd been commanded. Ephesians 6:13b says, "having done all, to stand" (NKJV). Have we done "all?" Have we done what we were supposed to do, or have we quit too soon?

We see in 2 Kings 5, where Naaman, the captain of the host of the king of Syria, contracted leprosy. He went to see the prophet Elisha, but the prophet wouldn't even come outside the house to greet him. He sent word for Naaman to go and dip in the Jordan River seven times, and he would be clean.

Why did Naaman have to dip seven times? The reason was simply because that was what God had said—that is why it had to be done seven times. It matters not if we think six times will be enough. I am pressing this point because I do not want you to make some of the mistakes that I have made. Just because I may get tired washing five times doesn't make it okay to quit early if God told me to do something seven times. We must be fully obedient and not give up too soon. Obedience to God isn't based on doing what I think or feel should be done. If God said seven times, then it is seven times.

We must be fully obedient and not give up too soon.

Chapter 5
No Compromise

You may remember a time when you first got a word from God about a situation. You were probably so excited that you may have risen earlier in the morning to read the Bible, pray, and lay your case out before God. Don't quit too soon or compromise on the promise if you don't see results as quickly as you anticipated when you first got your word.

In the story from 2 Kings 3:6-18 about the three kings who ran out of water crossing the desert, the word from the Lord was "'Make this valley full of ditches.' For thus says the Lord: 'You shall not see wind, nor shall you see rain; yet that valley shall be filled with water, so that you, your cattle, and your animals may drink'" (2 Kings 3:16-17, NKJV). Remember, God said they would not feel any wind or see any rain! It was going to happen, but they wouldn't see the *process* of it happening. God is looking for faith.

In Naaman's story, found in 2 Kings chapter 5, Naaman was upset because the prophet didn't even see him in person. Instead, the prophet sent instructions for how the leprosy would be healed, and it wasn't to happen in a way that Naaman had expected. The passage reads:

> But Naaman stormed off, grumbling, "Why couldn't he come out and talk to me? I thought for sure he would stand in front of me and pray to the Lord his God, then wave his hand over my skin and cure me. What about the Abana River or the Pharpar River?

Those rivers in Damascus are just as good as any river
in Israel. I could have washed in them and been
cured." His servants went over to him and said, "Sir, if
the prophet had told you to do something difficult, you
would have done it. So why don't you do what he
said? Go wash and be cured." Naaman walked down to
the Jordan; he waded out into the water and stooped
down in it seven times, just as Elisha had told him.
Right away, he was cured, and his skin became as
smooth as a child's. (2 Kings 5:11-14, CEV)

What if, in his frustration, Naaman had stopped washing on
the fifth time? God does not want us focusing on our
strengths, talents, or abilities. God wants us to focus only on
Him and what He has commanded us to do. Don't
compromise by being less than fully obedient. Where's your
faith?

*God doesn't want us focusing on our own strengths,
talents, or abilities. He wants us to focus only on Him.*

God is looking for faith. It's not as though Naaman
saw a little change in his skin at five dips. He saw nothing!
Maybe God knows that if we see a little change, we will get
satisfied with the progress and not continue.

I have, at times, found this to be true in my life. I begin
thinking, "I can live with this. I don't need to have it all." It's
as though we talk ourselves into having self-righteous
thoughts about not being greedy and not needing all that God
has promised. It's not about being greedy, however, it's about

doing what God says to do. The devil is always there to get us to compromise. DON'T

My experience is that the enemy will often come and try to get me to compromise for less than the big dreams God has given me. I begin to think that my dreams are so big and that maybe I really don't need all that I'm dreaming about possessing. The devil will always give you something lesser to look at—a comparison that is shy of all that God wants for you.

Think about the Israelites and the Promised Land. In Deuteronomy 1:8, Moses tells the Israelites regarding the Promised Land that God said, "I am giving all of it to you! Go in and possess it, for it is the land the Lord promised to your ancestors Abraham, Isaac, and Jacob, and all of their descendants" (TLB). They had a promise, yet two of the tribes chose to settle on the other side. This story is found in Numbers:

> When Israel arrived in the land of Jazar and Gilead, the tribes of Reuben and Gad (who had large flocks of sheep) noticed what wonderful sheep country it was. So they came to Moses and Eleazar the priest and the other tribal leaders and said, "The Lord has used Israel to destroy the population of this whole countryside . . .. And it is all wonderful sheep country, ideal for our flocks. Please let us have this land as our portion instead of the land on the other side of the Jordan River." (TLB)

They had a promise, but they compromised all that God had for them, the best, and settled for less-than-the-best. It's not

18

about what you feel you need now. We have no idea what God has planned in the future, and we are blessed so that we can be a blessing to others. Don't settle for less than your promise. Don't compromise.

Don't settle for less than God's best for you.

Later, after Moses had died, Joshua had the huge task of leading an entire nation into the Promised Land. The Lord told Joshua, "Above all, be strong and very courageous to carefully observe the whole instruction My servant Moses commanded you. Do not turn from it to the right or the left, so that you will have success wherever you go" (Joshua 1:7, HCSB). He continues in verse 8 of Joshua 1, saying "This book of instruction must not depart from your mouth; you are to recite it day and night so that you may carefully observe everything written in it. For *then* you will prosper and succeed in whatever you do" (HCSB).

Like Joshua, you have the task of leading your family into God's promises. How do you do this? Choose to be strong and meditate on the Word of God so that you can do all that it says, *then* you will have success. Success doesn't come until you have done the "*then.*" Be strong and courageous. Meditate on the Word—on your promises. Obey His instructions. Don't settle for less.

Chapter 6
Speaking Power and Following God's Word

God has not changed. Hebrews 13:8 says, "Jesus Christ is the same yesterday, today, and forever" (NKJV). The principles gleaned from the examples in the Word, wherever they are located, are just as relevant today as they were when they first occurred.

We've looked at some examples of obtaining promises in the Old Testament. Now let's look in the New Testament. In the book of Mark, chapter 11, there is a story about a fig tree. Jesus was hungry, and, in the distance, He saw a fig tree with leaves. When He got to the tree, He saw that there were no figs on it at all. Verse 14 of Mark 11 says, "In response Jesus said to it, 'Let no one eat fruit from you ever again.' And His disciples heard it" (NKJV). The next morning, Jesus and His disciples passed back by the fig tree and noticed that it had dried up from the roots (Mark 11:20, NKJV).

When Peter noticed it, he called it to Jesus's attention. Mark 11:22 records Jesus's response:

> So Jesus answered and said to them, "Have faith in God. For assuredly, I say to you, whoever says to this mountain, 'Be removed and be cast into the sea,' and does not doubt in his heart, but believes that those things he says will be done, he will have whatever he says." (NKJV)

Jesus's lesson to the disciples about the fig tree was about speaking power—speaking to your mountains, your situations.

Mark 11:14 (KJV) says, "And *Jesus answered and said unto it*, No man eat fruit of thee hereafter for ever. And his disciples heard it." He answered *it*—the tree! That tree had been speaking.

You may feel silly speaking to a situation. It does not matter how you feel about opening your mouth and addressing a problem, however, because the problem speaks to you! I'm sure that I am not the only one who ever opens a bill and it begins to talk to me. Things can talk. Situations and problems can speak loud and clear. Just like that tree had been talking to Jesus, you can ride by a gas station and the sign bearing the cost of gas talks!

But Jesus said for us to talk to our situations. We must be speaking *to* our mountain; and don't get confused—there is a difference between "to" and "about." So many times, we spend time talking *about* our problems rather than speaking *to* them and telling them to change.

Speak to your mountain!

Speak to those mountains! Say, "Gas prices, you are coming down, in Jesus's name. I speak to the greed demons and principalities driving the prices up." Don't be talking *about* the prices—talk *to* them!

Speak to that devil that is trying to take your family. Talk to that demonic influence trying to work on your teenager. Say to that influence, "You will bow your knee. Pack your junk and get out of my house!"

So often we want to stand without speaking. We must speak to the mountain. You can't just think that you have God's word on a matter and there's nothing else you need to do about a situation. Speak to that mountain of adversity. Call to it to be removed and cast into the sea, and do not doubt.

Beyond just speaking to our mountains, we must follow God's Word. In Mark 11:25, Jesus said, "And when you stand praying, forgive if you have anything against anyone, so that your Father who is in Heaven may also forgive you your sins" (MEV). Jesus said that we are to forgive, and it doesn't matter if we feel like it or not. Unless you do all God says, you will not have results!

Follow God's Word – all of it.

Forgiving someone for what they've done doesn't necessarily mean that we unload on the person we are forgiving. We are to be led by the Holy Ghost, who may tell us just to release it in our heart. The enemy will do anything he can to bring offense, and unforgiveness is one of the greatest hindrances to people receiving from God. No matter what the words or actions were that were done to you, the greatest joy and freedom will come from just letting it go. Do what God says to do—follow His Word.

Unforgiveness is one of the greatest hindrances to people receiving from God.

We can't follow God's Word if we don't know what His Word says! Just as God spoke to Joshua, we, too, must meditate on the Word. "Meditate on it day and night so that you may act carefully according to all that is written in it. For then you will make your way successful, and you will be wise" (Joshua 1:8, MEV).

We can't follow God's Word if we don't know what it says!

It is important that we keep our minds filled with the Word, not with the situations and circumstances with which we face. We must meditate on God's evidence—the truth of the Word; not the world's evidence—what we see in the natural. That's what faith is. Faith is God's evidence. Hebrews 11:1 says, "Now faith is the substance of things hoped for, the evidence of things not seen" (KJV).

We don't need the world's evidence: evidence about upheaval in the economy or evidence about political disturbances. We need God's evidence: faith that calls those things that are not as though they are. Romans 4:17 says, "God, who . . . calls things into existence that do not exist" (HCSB).

Until I am standing in the place of faith, I will have no rest. Are we still pressing? God says He wants men to always pray and not faint, lose heart, give up, or throw in the towel. We don't pray just until we think it is sufficient, we pray until God says it's sufficient.

In Luke 5, there is a story about the disciples who had been fishing all night with no success. In verse 5, Simon Peter responds to Jesus's command to cast out his net again. Peter said, ". . . 'Master, we have toiled all night and caught nothing; nevertheless at Your word I will let down the net'" (Luke 5:5, NJKV). All it took was for Jesus to speak the word and for them to obey and follow it.

Have you come up empty lately? You may be tired, but don't quit. You may not have seen success yet, but don't give up. Follow God's Word; don't throw in the towel. Keep on pressing and standing in faith.

All it may take is obedience to one word from Jesus.
Follow His Word.

Do you want to see results? You must push past your tiredness and past what the devil wants your breaking point to be. You must press until you hit your spiritual second wind. When you think you must give up, just reach down on the inside, and think on God's Word. A new strength will hit you. Then, having done all, stand.

Chapter 7
Be Prepared to Work

You may say that all of this sounds like work, and that's not what you expected. There is no work to salvation, but many times there is work required to press in and claim a promise. James, in the New Testament, says that faith without works is dead (James 2:17). Jesus has already done all He will do, but we have some work to do on our side.

There are so many examples in the Word about needing to work toward our promises and goals. The apostle Paul said, "I don't mean to say I am perfect. I haven't learned all I should even yet, but I keep working toward that day when I will finally be all that Christ saved me for and wants me to be" (Philippians 3:12, TLB). In that same passage of Scripture, Paul continues, "I press toward the goal for the prize of the upward call of God in Christ Jesus" (Philippians 3:14, NKJV).

Another example found in the Bible is when Peter steps out of the boat to walk on the water to Jesus. Matthew 14:24 reads, "But the boat was now in the middle of the sea, tossed by the waves, for the wind was contrary" (NKJV). The wind and waves did not stop when Jesus gave Peter the word to come to Him. There was no little paved road that appeared so that he could walk out to Jesus. When he stepped out, the wind was still howling, and the waves were still whipping. He had to step out at the word of Jesus on faith!

In John chapter 2, Jesus was with His disciples at a wedding in Cana of Galilee. His mother was there also. Jesus's mother came to Him and told Him that the bridal party had run out of wine. Scripture says, "Jesus said to her, 'Woman, what does your concern have to do with Me? My hour has not yet come'" (John 2:4, NKJV). His mother was totally unaffected by His statement. Knowing who He was, she replied to the servants, "Whatever He says to you, do it" (John 2:5, NKJV).

Jesus's mother understood who Jesus was. It didn't matter what Jesus told the servants. No matter how foolish it sounded, she knew they needed to do what He said. John 2:6-10 records what happened:

> Now there were set there six waterpots of stone, according to the manner of purification of the Jews, containing twenty or thirty gallons apiece. Jesus said to them [the servants], "Fill the waterpots with water." And they filled them up to the brim. And He said to them, "Draw some out now, and take it to the master of the feast." And they took it. When the master of the feast had tasted the water that was made wine, and did not know where it came from (but the servants who had drawn the water knew), the master of the feast called the bridegroom. And he said to him, "Every man at the beginning sets out the good wine, and when the guests have well drunk, then the inferior. You have kept the good wine until now!" (NKJV)

Putting water in the pots seemed foolish. It made no sense at all. That mattered not. Whatever He says to you, do it.

No matter how foolish it sounds, be prepared to do the work He calls you to do.

Jesus is all about taking care of people. He told His followers in the book of Matthew, ". . . I assure you: Whatever you did for one of the least of these brothers of Mine, you did for Me" (Matthew 25:40, HCSB). The things that Jesus calls us to do, we need to be about doing them. He calls us to work for a purpose.

Works are an expression of our faith. We don't work to get God's attention, we work because He has already given us His attention. James 2:14-18 reads:

> What good is it, my brothers, if someone says he has faith but does not have works? Can his faith save him? If a brother or sister is without clothes and lacks daily food and one of you says to them, "Go in peace, keep warm, and eat well," but you don't give them what the body needs, what good is it? In the same way faith, if it doesn't have works, is dead by itself. But someone will say, "You have faith, and I have works." Show me your faith without works, and I will show you faith from my works. (HCSB)

We don't do works to get into Heaven, we do works because we are already on the way. It's the same with praise. We don't praise to try to get in, we praise because we are already in.

Works are an important expression of our faith. Why? Because the world cannot just look at you or me and see our faith, but they can see the results of our faith. That's part of the purpose of works. Peter could say he had faith to get out of the boat, but no one believed him until he stepped out. When he stepped out, they realized that he had water-walking faith.

The world cannot just look at you and see your faith, but they can see the results of your faith.

We can talk all we'd like about faith, but will the people we spend time with know that we have water-walking faith? They will never know it unless they see us walking on the water. Scripture says that we are foolish if we think that we have faith without doing what God calls us to do. James 2:20-26 says the following:

> Fool! When will you ever learn that "believing" is useless without *doing* what God wants you to? Faith that does not result in good deeds is not real faith. Don't you remember that even our father Abraham was declared good because of what he *did* when he was willing to obey God, even if it meant offering his son Isaac to die on the altar? You see, he was trusting God so much that he was willing to do whatever God told him to; his faith was made complete by what he did – by his actions, his good deeds. And so it happened just as the Scriptures say, that Abraham trusted God, and the Lord declared him good in God's sight, and he was even called "the friend of God." So you see, a man is saved by what he does, as well as by what he believes. Rahab, the prostitute, is another example of this. She was saved because of what she did when she hid those messengers and sent them

safely away by a different road. Just as the body is
dead when there is no spirit in it, so faith is dead if it is
not the kind that results in good deeds. (TLB)
Be prepared to work—to do all that God tells you to do to see
your promise come to pass. Our faith is expressed by what we
do. How big is your faith? Show us!

*People will never know what we believe
unless they see us doing what God commands.*

Chapter 8
Don't Compare Yourself to Others

Have we done all? We may have received a prophetic word and certainly do have a Book full of promises that are "yes" and "amen" to those who believe, but are we doing all that we need to do? It is very important to understand that my "all" may be different from your "all." I may stop at five dips, when you have been asked to go to seven.

You cannot stop at what someone else has done and expect to get the same results that they have gotten. You have no idea what God may have said for them to do just like they don't know what God told *you* to do. While it is true that we live in a competitive world, we cannot let that competitive nature penetrate our spiritual lives or the church.

You cannot base your obedience on someone else's command and expect to get the same results.

We may think we know how another person lives, but we only know what they show us. All you know is what they let you see. You may say, "I did what they did, and nothing happened for me." You don't really know what they did. You only know what they told you and what you saw. You don't know the hours they prayed, what they sowed, or even the years they stood on their promise.

Sometimes, when we see a brother or sister get a blessing, recognition, or promotion, we become envious rather than rejoicing with them. Be wise and come against those ungodly thoughts. James 3:13-18 says:

> If you are wise and understand God's ways, prove it by living an honorable life, doing good works with the humility that comes from wisdom. But if you are bitterly jealous and there is selfish ambition in your heart don't cover up the truth with boasting and lying. For jealousy and selfishness are not God's kind of wisdom. Such things are earthly, unspiritual, and demonic. For wherever there is jealousy and selfish ambition, there you will find disorder and evil of every kind. But the wisdom from above is first of all pure. It is also peace loving, gentle at all times, and willing to yield to others. It is full of mercy and the fruit of good deeds. It shows no favoritism and is always sincere. And those who are peacemakers will plant seeds of peace and reap a harvest of righteousness. (NLT)

You may say that you prayed as much as they did, but you have no real way of knowing. Nobody knows the seeds they planted or how they stood on their promise but God, and God does know. He knows what you have done as well, and how you have worked. He keeps a record. Hebrews 6:10 tells us, "For God is not unjust. He will not forget how hard you have worked for Him and how you have shown your love to Him by caring for other believers, as you still do" (NLT).

As believers, we must put a value on and have an appreciation for the gifts that others have. Never allow envy or jealousy to come between you and anyone else. If I became jealous of the church pianist or a vocalist, then I have not positioned myself for their gift to pull me to a higher level of praise. My depreciation of their gift will only hurt me. Appreciate all the gifts in the body of Christ, because every joint and part of the body has a supply. Ephesians 4:15-16 explains:

> But instead we will remain strong and always sincere in our love as we express the truth. All our direction and ministries will flow from Christ and lead us deeper into Him, the anointed Head of His body, the church. For his "body" has been formed in His image and is closely joined together and constantly connected as one. And every member has been given divine gifts to contribute to the growth of all; and as these gifts operate effectively throughout the whole body, we are built up and made perfect in love. (TPT)

So it is good to choose to thank God for the visionaries who receive the plans of God and the skills of those who carry out those plans.

Chapter 9
Pure Offerings, Worship, and Attitude

There is a story in the Bible about a poor widow who gave two mites, or lepta, into the offering box at the temple. To understand better the value of a mite, the footnotes in Scripture say that it was about six minutes of an average daily wage (1/64 of a day's wage), almost nothing in value. The story is found in Luke:

> Jesus was in the temple, observing all the wealthy wanting to be noticed as they came with their offerings. He noticed a very poor widow dropping two small copper coins in the offering box. "Listen to me," He said. "This poor widow has given a larger offering than any of the wealthy. For the rich only gave out of their surplus, but she sacrificed out of her poverty and gave to God all that she had to live on." (Luke 21:1-4, TPT)

What the widow gave may have been small in actual number, but what she sacrificed was great. She gave all she had. Numbers have nothing to do with sacrifice. It's all about what the cost is to you. In 2 Samuel 24:24, David said that he would never offer anything to the Lord that did not cost him something, because then it would not be a true offering.

Numbers have nothing to do with sacrifice.

It is obedience, faith, and sacrifice that gets God's attention. The two mites which held so little earthly value got the Lord's attention. Never despise what you have in your hand to give. Never let the devil tell you that you have nothing to give or nothing to offer. Don't ever devalue your seed. Every seed is precious.

In Malachi, chapter 1, the Lord is chastising the priests for presenting to Him defiled offerings. Rather than offering the best and the unblemished, they were offering the blind, sick, and lame animals. This was dishonoring of the Lord's name. They had gotten the attitude that any old thing would do. This was a serious situation to the Lord. The Lord challenged them to offer their polluted offerings to their governor to see if he would be pleased with that kind of giving and accept them favorably. He said, "Just try giving those animals to your governor. That certainly wouldn't please him or make him want to help you" (Malachi 1:8, CEV).

The Lord even said that He wished there was just one among them who would shut the door and not even let those kinds of offerings into His house (Malachi 1:10). That is a strong word! A pure offering is what the Lord desires. Malachi 1:11-13 reads:

> "But my name will be honored by the Gentiles from morning till night. All around the world they will offer sweet incense and pure offerings in honor of My name. For My name shall be great among the nations," says the Lord Almighty. "But you dishonor it, saying that My altar is not important and encouraging people to bring cheap, sick animals to offer to Me on it. You say,

'Oh, it's too difficult to serve the Lord and do what He asks.' And you turn up your noses at the rules He has given you to obey. Think of it! Stolen animals, lame and sick—as offerings to God! Should I accept such offerings as these?" asks the Lord. (TLB)

He is the Lord Almighty, worthy of *our* very best, just as He gave us *His* very best. And He will hold nothing good back from us. Psalm 84:11 says, "no good thing will He withhold from those who walk uprightly" (NKJV). But the choice to give Him our best is ours to make. What are you doing, what are you giving to the One who gave His all for you? What you have in your hand has value.

The choice to give God our best is ours to make.

Just as a pure offering is what we should be honoring the Lord with, we are also to give Him the purest of our praises! Hebrews 13:15 says, "Through Him, then, let us continually offer to God the sacrifice of praise, which is the fruit of our lips, giving thanks to His name" (MEV). We may think that we have done all that God has asked, but are we offering praise to Him? We may have our finances in proper order, but where is our heart?

At church, when it comes time for praise and worship, if our heart is focused on anything other than Jesus, what kind of sacrifice are we making? If we are already thinking about Monday, are we not still offering a lame sacrifice? Is it not still a polluted sacrifice if our thoughts are on some issue that may happen next week or next month, and our heart and attention are not focused on Him?

When we enter church, we must leave the economy, our job, social statuses, and anything else that would keep us from focusing on Him outside those doors. When we enter in, we need to be *ready* to enter in. Psalm 100:4 says, "Enter into His gates with thanksgiving, and into His courts with praise. Be thankful to Him, and bless His name" (NKJV). We need to focus on the reason we are worshipping.

One of the keys to having done all and seeing breakthrough come to us is in the realm of praise and worship. God is looking for a pure heart. In John 4:23, Jesus says, "But the hour is coming, and now is, when the true worshipers will worship the Father in spirit and truth; for the Father is seeking such to worship Him" (NKJV). Our praise must come from a focused, pure heart.

We must return to a level of praise that is pure and untainted—including not being distracted by things we see happening during the worship service. What difference does it make for us if, when we are worshipping God in church, one person is running around, and another is lying out on the floor? We should not focus on them or question why the person is running around. How they choose to worship, or how the Lord calls them to express their worship has nothing to do with anyone else.

We must do *all* that God calls *us* to do—as must they. Their "all" is different from my "all!" I must also refuse to step into criticism. As soon as I become critical about what someone else is doing, I have polluted my own praise.

36

We must do all that God calls us to do.

By the same token, if you take off running around and God did not tell you to run, you have polluted your praise. If you raise your hands just because the person next to you raises theirs, you have done so for the wrong reason. Worship God as only you can do, in the way He calls *you* to worship—purely from your heart, not because of what someone else is doing. 1 John 3:1 reads, "Consider how much love the Father has given to us, that we should be called children of God" (MEV). Think about how much love He has for us, and that will help to lavish our praise and adoration back on Him in worship. God is looking for a pure heart and pure worship—focused, lavished love on Him.

My all is different from yours. We must be utterly transparent with the Holy Ghost, in-line and in-tune with Him. We can sing about how we want to give our all, but the time has come to live what we have been singing. It is time for the church to be walking in the results of the power of the Word of God, doing all He has called us to do.

Psalm 100 tells us to make a joyful noise unto the Lord, to serve Him with gladness, and to come before His presence with singing. God made us. Any man who says he is a self-made man is deceived. Psalm 100:3 says, "Know that the Lord, He is God; it is He who has made us, and not we ourselves; we are His people, and the sheep of His pasture" (MEV). In this Psalm, we are told to enter His gates with thanksgiving, and that means leaving our thoughts of the world and its problems outside.

Having Done All, Stand

When we come into His presence, our heart and attitudes should be right. We should have an expectation of God doing something amazing in our hearts and lives. We should realize that we are in the presence of the King, and in His presence are miracles and unending possibility for change.

In the presence of His power and glory, all things are possible! In Matthew 19:26, Jesus said, "With men this is impossible, but with God all things are possible" (NKJV). Keep this in mind during worship and it will help you focus on the only One who can make the impossible possible. Psalm 100:4-5 says, "Enter into His gates with thanksgiving, and into His courts with praise. Be thankful to Him, and bless His name. For the Lord is good; His mercy is everlasting, and His truth endures to all generations" (NKJV). He alone is worthy of all our praise and we have much for which to be thankful. We would be wise to keep our offerings, worship, and attitudes pure before Him while we stand.

Worship the One who can make all things possible.

Chapter 10
Complete Obedience

If we haven't done all that God has asked us to do, we will frustrate our own faith. I heard Pastor Willie George tell a story once that impacted my life tremendously. He had received a powerfully prophetic word that God was about to bless him with an awesome children's ministry. He went home and sat by the telephone. Nothing happened.

As time went by, he began to question God about why nothing was happening. God then spoke to him and told him nothing was happening because Pastor Willie had done nothing. God asked him what he planned to do when he went out to do children's ministry. God said, "Do you plan to take the materials that belong to the church, leaving them with nothing, while you go out ministering to all those other churches? Get your own stuff!"

He immediately asked the Lord what he should do. The Lord instructed him on how to get the money. Pastor Willie constructed an entire portable stage complete with puppets, and as soon as he had finished, his phone started ringing. It wasn't too long before he had as many as 3,000 young people each week! But nothing happened until he had done all he was supposed to do. During the time when he was sitting and waiting on the phone to ring, all he was doing was opening himself up for frustration and questioning the word of the Lord. He had done nothing to prepare for the word he'd been given.

Right now may be your preparation time. You can dream until Jesus comes back, but if you are not getting storehouses ready and doing all that He has instructed you to do, you are setting yourself up for frustration.

Preparation, not dreaming, is needed to obey.

Getting a prophetic word is exciting. Hearing a story like Pastor Willie's helps us to break out of complacency and get in-tune with the Holy Ghost to find out if we have missed any instructions! Ask the Lord if you have dropped the ball anywhere, left something undone, or failed to prepare in some area. Could any of those be the reason the door I have been waiting to open has remained closed? Have I gotten my affairs in order like I need to?

Again, if He says dig ditches, then dig ditches. If He says to gather empty vessels, then gather empty vessels. If He says dip seven times, then dip seven times. If He says to pray, then pray. Whatever He says to do, do it.

I sometimes still struggle with trying to figure everything out. The old nature rises and tells me that what God is asking doesn't make sense. God doesn't ask for us to understand or to help Him. He asks us to obey Him.

We may ask our children to clean their room and make their bed. They may respond, "Why have I got to make my bed? No one is coming over and I'm getting back into the bed tonight anyway!" But you want the bed made. It's the responsibility of the child to obey the one in authority, whether they understand why or even agree.

Complete Obedience

God expects us to obey, not understand His command.

Parents demand obedience without a child needing to understand the reasoning behind the demand. Ephesians 6:1 (KJV) is a verse easily recognized, "Children, obey your parents in the Lord: for this is right." Another version of that same verse reads, "Children, obey your parents as you would the Lord, because this is right" (HCSB). This puts a greater responsibility on the parents to make sure children learn to obey without question or retort, as they are training their children to also obey the Lord when He speaks to them.

There are blessings that come with complete obedience. Deuteronomy 5:33 reads, "Follow the whole instruction the Lord your God has commanded you, so that you may live, prosper, and have a long life in the land you will possess" (HCSB). Just as parents require children to be fully obedient, we have a heavenly Father whose ways are much higher than our ways, and He requires complete obedience of His children as well.

There are blessings that come with complete obedience.

Chapter 11
Give Thanks

Giving thanks isn't just a concept reserved for November. It is a concept that should be infused into every prayer we offer up. Philippians 4:4-7 reads:

> Rejoice in the Lord always. Again I will say, rejoice! Let your gentleness [graciousness, forbearance, unselfishness] be known to all men. The Lord is at hand. Be anxious for nothing, but in everything by prayer and supplication, with thanksgiving, let your requests be made known to God; and the peace of God, which surpasses all understanding, will guard your hearts and minds through Christ Jesus. (NKJV)

The Contemporary English Version of Philippians 4:6 says, "Don't worry about anything, but pray about everything. With thankful hearts offer up your prayers and requests to God." The Passion Translation puts it this way, "Don't be pulled in different directions or worried about a thing. Be saturated in prayer throughout each day, offering your faith-filled requests before God with overflowing gratitude. Tell Him every detail of your life" (Philippians 4:6, TPT). Thankfulness in prayer, not worry, is key.

We are not to be anxious about the price of gas, groceries, or slumps in the economy. He didn't say not to pray about it, He just said not to get caught up in worrying about it! We need to pray, but we do not need to be anxious. It is faith that moves God, not fear or worry.

Don't get caught up in worry. Pray with faith and thanksgiving.

Have we, with faith, given thanks? Have we shown Him an attitude of gratitude for what we already have? Did you thank God for the clean, hot water you had when you took your shower or even washed your hands? There are many people who do not have running water in the house, and untold numbers who do not have access to clean water at all. God is not against us making requests, but He wants our attitude to be right and pure.

Keeping our minds and hearts focused on the right things, with a thankful attitude, is a powerful thing. Philippians 4:8 reads:

> Finally, brethren, whatever things are true, whatever things are noble, whatever things are just, whatever things are pure, whatever things are lovely, whatever things are of good report, if there is any virtue and if there is anything praiseworthy—meditate on these things. (NKJV)

God is not going to ask you to do something that is not on this list. He won't ask you to do something false, immoral, or a cause of shame. That wouldn't be His character or of His nature. Remember—He is good, all the time!

You are His servant, and I am telling you that *whatever* He says to do, do it! If He says dig ditches, you best grab a shovel and get that dirt piling high until He says stop. If He says borrow vessels, not a few, then you best go and borrow lots of vessels. If He says fill up water pots, you fill up water pots.

When He says pray, you pray. When He says forgive, you forgive. If He says go cut the neighbor's grass, you go and cut the neighbor's grass. You never know the impact your obedience will have on others or on your own situation. If He says to give the lady at the McDonald's drive-through window all your change, you say, "Keep the change!" It may be only one dollar, but that may be all it takes to keep her from a breaking point.

You never know the impact your obedience will have on others or on your own situation.

It's not up to us to figure it out or to work it out. It doesn't have to make sense to you. If He tells you to do it, then just do it, whatever it is.

If you want someone to be there for your teenager when pressure comes on them in high school, college, or as a laborer, why don't you consider sowing a seed now in children's church or Sunday School? Don't try to put a demand on a seed that you have not put into the ground. Galatians 6:7 says, "Don't be deceived: God is not mocked. For whatever a man sows he will also reap" (HCSB).

Have you picked up a young person to get them to church or to youth group meetings? You cannot reap a seed you have not sown. Believe God to pay your light bill and someone else's this month. Pump your gas and fill another person's tank. You don't have to know them. You don't even have to say, "Jesus loves you!" Scripture says, "So we must not get tired of doing good, for we will reap at the proper time if we don't give up. Therefore, as we have opportunity, we must work for the good of all, especially for those who belong to the household of faith" (Galatians 6:9-10, HCSB). Let's not waste the opportunities we are given, instead choose to be thankful for them, and do all He calls you to do.

You cannot reap a seed you have not sown.

Chapter 12
Stay on the Wall

Nehemiah was an awesome servant of God, and his story is found in the Old Testament. Nehemiah wasn't a priest, he was a servant of an ungodly king. When Nehemiah heard about Jerusalem's wall being broken down and that the people there were in distress, he sought the Lord for direction on what he could do. Nehemiah chapter 1 records his prayer, and the last verse captures Nehemiah's submission and determination, "O Lord, please hear my prayer! Listen to the prayers of those of us who delight in honoring You. Please grant me success today by making the king favorable to me. Put it into his heart to be kind to me" (Nehemiah 1:11, NLT).

He received a word from God to go back and rebuild the walls of Jerusalem. After praying, he went to the king to get permission to do so. Not only did he get permission to go rebuild the wall, but the king wrote letters to have the supplies provided for him! You don't have to know anyone besides God. God can get you what you need. All you need is to know God Himself.

You don't have to know anyone but God. He is your source.

Like so many of us, Nehemiah hit some turbulence in this assignment. Just because we have a word from God does not mean everything will be smooth, and we will encounter no trouble. It also does not mean that everyone will be excited for us.

We read in Nehemiah 4, that Sanballat and Tobiah were two men who became very indignant about the wall rebuilding the Jews were doing. The devil used them against the Jews to verbally abuse and harass them. No matter what the Jews did, there was opposition from these men continually trying to put them down and antagonize them.

Despite the constant criticism, the Jews continued to work together reconstructing the wall. Nehemiah 4:6 says, "So we built the wall and the entire wall was joined together up to half its height, for the people had a mind to work" (NKJV). Not only did they have a mind to work, they *kept* a mind to work despite anything that was said or done to them. They were not pulled off-course, nor distracted from their purpose. They were letting nothing stop them; each had a made-up mind.

Don't let anything distract you from God's plan and purpose for your life.

Ignoring the naysayers didn't make them go away, however. Nehemiah 4:7-9 reads:

Now it happened, when Sanballat, Tobiah, the Arabs, the Ammonites, and the Ashdodites heard that the walls of Jerusalem were being restored and the gaps were beginning to be closed, that they became very angry, and all of them conspired together to come and attack Jerusalem and create confusion. Nevertheless

we made our prayer to our God, and because of them
we set a watch against them day and night.

The Jews continued working. As they continued, so did the
opposition. You cannot just make a wish that dispels all the
naysayers. Adversity can be beneficial. In fact, sometimes it's
not bad to have a little resistance so that we know what we are
made of. Anybody can accomplish a task if it is easy.

Sanballat and Tobias had conspired together to get an
army to come and attack the Jews and to create confusion to
stop the work. Nehemiah and the Jews took it all to God in
prayer, set up a watch against their enemies, and continued
pressing in and working. But the workers became a little
distracted because of the army coming against them. They
were not cleaning up after their work and the whole process
stagnated. In Nehemiah 4:10, "Judah said, 'The strength of the
laborers is failing and there is so much rubbish that we are not
able to build the wall'" (NJKV).

When God gives you an assignment to do, the enemy
will try to trip you up, distract you, and get you off-course.
Nehemiah 4:11 says, "And our adversaries said, 'They will
neither know nor see anything, till we come into their midst
and kill them and cause the work to cease'" (NKJV). The Jews
could see their enemy, and had that more on their minds than
the assignment that was before them.

*The enemy will always try to trip you up, distract you,
and get you off-course. Stay focused!*

Nehemiah positioned the Jews to face their enemy head on and reminded them Whose they were. Nehemiah 4:13-14 says:

> Therefore I positioned men behind the lower parts of the wall, at the openings; and I set the people according to their families, with their swords, their spears, and their bows. And I looked, and arose and said to the nobles, to the leaders, and to the rest of the people, "Do not be afraid of them. Remember the Lord, great and awesome, and fight for your brethren, your sons, your daughters, your wives, and your houses. And it happened, when our enemies heard that it was known to us, and that God had brought their plot to nothing, that all of us returned to the wall, everyone to his work." (NKJV)

It was as though there was a righteous indignation—they were ready to fight the enemy with their weapons. The stance to fight, the refusal to back down, the dismissal of fear, and the enemy's plot exposed by the Lord combined sent the enemy back. Nehemiah had set the defense.

When the enemies heard that their plan had been revealed to the Jews by God, they knew their plan would not prevail. The Jews returned to the wall, everyone to his own work. From that time on, Scripture says, half of the servants worked at construction, while the other half held the spears, shield, bows, and wore armor. They all worked with one hand, and with the other hand, held a weapon (Nehemiah 4:16-17).

From this scripture comes a great lesson for us: stay on your wall! We must stay on our assignment, on our purpose,

and on what God has told us to do. We must build but stay
vigilant at the same time. We cannot be so "building-minded"
that we drop our guard, nor can we be so "spiritually-minded"
that we stop all our work. There must be a balance in our lives.

Stay on your assignment and purpose from God.

The economy may be bad, but we cannot stay home
and pray all day. We must go to our job. At the same time, we
cannot get so locked up in our job that we forget to pray. We
must learn how to keep our faith in one hand and our spiritual
weapons in the other. We must not get distracted from the
purpose or assignment that God has given us. We must learn
how to stay on our appointed task and wear the spiritual armor
that God provided for us.

Ephesians 6:10-11, already quoted in this book, reads,
"Finally, my brethren, be strong in the Lord and in the power
of His might. Put on the whole armor of God, that you may be
able to stand against the wiles [tactics, strategies] of the devil"
(NKJV). Putting on the armor is part of the "all" that we need
to do in order to stand. Verses 14-18 lists each piece at our
disposal:

> Stand therefore, having girded your waist with truth,
> having put on the breastplate of righteousness, and
> having shod your feet with the preparation of the
> gospel of peace; above all, taking the shield of faith
> with which you will be able to quench all the fiery
> darts of the wicked one. And take the helmet of
> salvation, and the Sword of the Spirit, which is the

Word of God; praying always with all prayer and supplication in the Spirit, being watchful to this end with all perseverance and supplication for all the saints." (NKJV)

The next time you put your armor on, be sure you put it *all* on. Do not go out (spiritually speaking) streaking. Keep your loins girded with truth, so that when you open your mouth, you are speaking truth and not trash. We put on the breastplate of righteousness because we are walking in the righteousness of God. The world needs to see it. We shod our feet so that everywhere we go, the peace, power, and presence of God shows up. Our helmet must be on, so that our minds stay on Him.

With the shield and the sword, we can protect ourselves from the enemy's attacks and fight back with the Word of God. This armor is extremely important. Think about it the next time you believe you have done all and are attempting to stand. It will cause you to examine yourself and make sure you have done your all. We can stay on our wall, focused on our assignment, while armed and ready for spiritual battle.

Putting on the armor of God is part of the "all" we need to do in order to stand.

Chapter 13
God is in Control

There may be some turbulence in our world now, but we must remember that our Father is in control. We must have faith in Him. Have you ever seen the sign that says, "God is my co-pilot?" That is wrong thinking! If He is not the pilot, we need to swap seats quickly. Move over and put Him in the pilot's seat. We must put more confidence in *His* plan and *His* ability to get us where we're going rather than in *our* plan and ability.

God's plans and directions for our life need to be sought and then followed clearly. Let Him lead, and if you need help knowing what His plans are, ask for help from someone who could pray with you. In 1 Peter 5:5, we read, "Likewise you younger people, submit yourselves to your elders. Yes, all of you be submissive to one another, and be clothed with humility, for 'God resists the proud, but gives grace to the humble'" (NKJV). Many people do not get the help they need because of pride. There is nothing wrong with asking for prayer. You don't need to reveal every detail, but ask for prayer when you need help.

Let God lead you and don't let pride stop you from seeking help when you need it.

1 Peter 5:6-7 tells us to "Humble yourselves under the mighty hand of God, that He may exalt you in due time. Cast

all your care upon Him, because He cares for you" (MEV). The Lord also warns us in the verses that follow to "Be sober, be vigilant; because your adversary the devil walks about like a roaring lion, seeking whom he may devour" (1 Peter 5:8, NKJV). Scripture tells us to be sober-minded. If you have ever been around a person who is drunk, you realize they are unable to think straight. They often think they can drive safely, but they can't. They can't even walk straight, though they think they can. This is not a safe mental or physical state. We, too, must stay mentally alert so that we are aware of the tactics of the enemy.

The next verse says, "Resist him [the enemy], steadfast in the faith, knowing that the same sufferings are experienced by your brotherhood in the world" (1 Peter 5:9, NKJV). We *can* resist the enemy, stay strong, and encourage others to do the same. We do not have to go through difficulties alone, and we aren't alone in facing them—all our brothers and sisters in Christ face various struggles! There are others who have gone through situations just like yours. There may even be someone you know right now who is going through a situation similar to yours.

Sometimes we think that we are the only one going through temptations and trials, and the enemy can use that thought to bring torment. But Scripture tells us ". . . submit yourselves to God. Resist the devil, and he will flee from you" (James 4:7, MEV). As you are standing against the enemy, you can help other believers to stand strong as well.

There is peace that comes in knowing that we are not the only one having trouble. It's encouraging to know that we have not done some huge, terrible thing that has caused us to face a problem. But we do have an adversary looking for someone to devour (1 Peter 5:8). He will continue to push and push, especially on the weak or those who have not been in the Word. He will look for those who have their guard down or who have become a little distracted. Therefore, we can't ever let our guard down; we must stay focused on God's directions, spend time in the Word, and spend time praying.

A lack of time spent in prayer and in the Word may have caused our walls to have cracks, parts missing, or even be destroyed like the wall of Jerusalem in Nehemiah. Maybe we are listening to a little of the gossip at work or are beginning to believe some things being said about the boss. The boss may not be that bad but is being attacked by workers who want the boss's job. Perhaps they don't want to pay the price that was paid to get the job and think that gossip and stirring up strife will cause the boss to quit, leaving an opportunity for them to step in.

That's one way the enemy works. The adversary is looking for someone to take out. 1 Peter 5:9 says that we must resist him in the faith, and the instruction to do so wouldn't be in the Word as a command if it were impossible to accomplish. Staying in the Word equips us with the tools we need to defeat the enemy. Romans 10:17 says, "So then faith comes by hearing, and hearing by the word of God" (NKJV). We must stay in the Word to have our faith built up, and we must also stay in prayer. Jude 20 says, "But you, beloved, build yourselves up in your most holy faith. Pray in the Holy Spirit" (MEV).

We can resist the enemy, or it wouldn't be in the Word!

We must stay in that place of communion with God so that we can stay built up. This can be compared to what happens in our physical bodies. When we get busy, don't eat properly, or take good care of our bodies, we let our immunity get low. When this happens, we do not have the resistance to infection that we need. In the same manner, we must keep our spiritual immunity built up, so that we have the resistance we need to stand against the devourer when he comes.

God is in control, and He has a plan. He knows us better than we know ourselves. Sometimes it is difficult to grow without a little adversity. People who work out to build physical strength and endurance often use weights or other resistance methods to cause their muscles to grow. We can grow even during difficulty. Thankfully, we read in 1 Peter 5:10, "But after you have suffered a little while, the God of all grace, who has called us to His eternal glory through Christ Jesus, will restore, support, strengthen, and establish you" (MEV). When He says suffer, He is referring to endurance.

We may say we never want any adversity but if we don't have any adversity to push against, we may never get any stronger. We say we want to move up to the next level, but if we don't have the strength to handle that level, God would be cruel to put us there. If you are just hanging on or having trouble in the place where you are now, what will you do on the next level? If God were to promote you to a higher level without any tests or proving time for the strength you need, it might crush you.

Having Done All, Stand

If we don't have any adversity to push against, we may never get any stronger.

       As you are standing, trust that God is in control. Where you currently are may not be where you want to be, but perhaps what you are enduring is training you for your next position. He will not promote you where He cannot sustain you, and He won't place you before you are ready.

Chapter 14
Do Not Become Distracted

We cannot let upheavals that are going on in the world override our faith or our purpose. We cannot become so distracted at our job that we are no longer being a light. We must not find ourselves participating in negative conversations. I realize that we cannot continually be preaching Jesus. We are on a time clock, and we must render to Caesar what is his. However, we must resist getting drawn into negative conversations about what is going on in the office, in our nation, or in the world. Our conversation must be turned away from the problems that are prevalent and center on how good God is. We should remind others that He will get us through whatever the turbulence is around us.

Don't become distracted – focus on God's goodness.

Song of Solomon 2:15 says that it's "the little foxes that spoil the vineyards" (MEV). Remember that the devil often uses "little foxes," seemingly minor issues, to get us distracted from spending time in the Word or in prayer. We must take a lesson from Nehemiah, who stayed focused even though he had to work with weapons in his hands. We must learn how to keep building without distractions yet stay armed in the Spirit. We must learn to stay focused on our specific task, letting nothing stop us from complete obedience.

We must stay focused and armed in the Spirit.

When we are focused, we can be more effective with our time. Productivity – using our time efficiently – is connected to our character. When our character is complete, we will not be unfruitful. 2 Peter 1:5-8 tells us:

> For this reason make every effort to add virtue to your faith; and to your virtue, knowledge; and to your knowledge, self-control; and to your self-control, patient endurance; and to your patient endurance, godliness; and to your godliness, brotherly kindness; and to your brotherly kindness, love. For if these things reside in you and abound, they ensure that you will neither be useless nor unfruitful in the knowledge of our Lord Jesus Christ. (MEV)

As we add to our character, we will be useful and fruitful in the Kingdom.

Productivity is connected to our character.

The word unfruitful in 1 Peter 5:8 means idle. You can be busy but not fruitful. We don't want to be busy without being productive. An example of this is when you have a day in which you run from sun up to sun down, but you don't seem to accomplish anything. That's a busy day, but not a fruitful day. Time is extremely important. It's one thing that you cannot get back. Wisdom would have us use it as efficiently as possible, so it's important not to get distracted.

2 Peter 1: 9-12 continues the instruction, saying:

But the one who lacks these things is blind and shortsighted because he has forgotten that he was cleansed from his former sins. Therefore, brothers, diligently make your calling and election sure. For if you do these things, you will never stumble. For in this way the entrance into the eternal kingdom of our Lord and Savior Jesus Christ will be abundantly provided for you. Therefore I will not be negligent to always remind you of these things, though you know them and are established in the truth that is present with you. (MEV)

This instruction reminds us to be sure of what we are supposed to be doing. Stay focused—don't get distracted. If we stay focused, we will not stumble in our calling. We already know all these things, but we need to be reminded so that we don't let our guard down. We never want to allow the enemy to find a hole in our armor. We do not want the adversary to find an open door into our lives or our family. We must help each other remember not to give up on God's plan and our purpose until the assignments given are accomplished. Then, having done all, we can stand.

Praying for our spiritual family helps us feel empowered in that we are doing something that can make tremendous impact. James 5:16b says, "The earnest prayer of a righteous person has great power and produces wonderful results" (NLT). When you pray for someone, it makes a difference! It also helps those working to obtain promises know that there is someone standing with them.

Praying for others is empowering because it makes a tremendous impact!

It can be as simple as asking our brother or sister in Christ how they are coming with their promise, or we can tell them how we are doing with ours. We can ask if there is something they need agreement in prayer about, and share with them our needs, as well. It may be a problem as simple as having difficulty getting children to mind. Partnering in prayer doesn't have to only be about a heavy spiritual assignment. We can pray against the little distractions, the "little foxes" too! It's good to stay aware that we are all going through something so that we can be supportive of each other.

Just because you are not preaching to thousands does not mean that your assignment is not equally important. Each person has a specific task to complete—their own God-given purpose. It is up to us to make the most of what we have so that we can do all that we need to do.

Each person has a specific assignment for a given purpose and must choose to be productive and effective.

There is a parable in Matthew 25:14-30 that is known as the Parable of the Talents. Jesus tells that there was a man who was traveling who left his financial affairs in the care of three chosen servants. He gave specific amounts of money to each of them (one was given five talents, another two talents, and the last he gave one talent), and when he returned from his journey, two of the servants had doubled the money with which their master entrusted them, but the last servant, out of fear, buried the one talent left with him and thus made no profit.

The two servants who were productive with what was given them were each praised by their master. "'Wonderful!' his master replied. 'You are a good and faithful servant. I left you in charge of only a little, but now I will put you in charge of much more. Come and share in my happiness!'" (Matthew 25:21, CEV). God will speak in the same manner to the person who is effective with the two talents given them as He will to the one to whom was effective with more. He will say, "Well done, good and faithful servant!" God just wants us to be faithful with what we have been given.

Peter said in 1 Peter 1:12 that as long as he lived, he would continue to stir up those around him in the faith and put them in remembrance of the things of God. Undoubtedly, the believers were going through turbulence. We must also do this for each other. Try calling or sending a text to folks in your church or study group just to see how they are doing and to encourage them in the Lord. This would be a simple way to begin.

In the parable of the wheat and the tares, found in Matthew 13, Jesus explains another principle of the kingdom of Heaven. Verses 24-28 reads:

> He told them another parable, saying, "The kingdom of heaven is like a man who sowed good seed in his field. But while men slept, his enemy came and sowed weeds among the wheat and went away. But when the shoots had sprung up and produced fruit, the weeds

also appeared. So the servants of the landowner came and said to him, 'Sir, did you not sow good seed in your field? Then where did the weeds come from?' He said to them, "An enemy did this." (MEV)

This is what happens to us when we become distracted, and the enemy takes advantage of us. We end up reaping something we didn't plant because we were distracted from our purpose. We must remain watchful—vigilant.

When we are on guard, we recognize the enemy and can stop him when he tries to come in. When someone begins to gossip about a brother, we can refuse to hear and receive it. And it doesn't matter if what is being said is true or not! In Philippians 4:8, the Bible says, "whatever things are of good report . . . think on these things" (MEV) and that is what we should do. Even if it is truthful, gossiping is not giving a good report.

Stay focused on what God has called you to do so that you can be the most productive about your assignment. Stand with your brothers and sisters in prayer and look for ways to encourage one another. Stay focused—don't let anything distract you. God gave your assignment to you for a reason, and we must do all we can to see our purposes and promises fulfilled.

Chapter 15
Satan Never Gives Up–Neither Should We

The devil is very subtle, and he will keep working to trip us up until he finds what works. When you have a new baby who needs rest, you will sing a lullaby or do whatever it takes to get them to sleep. When my son was a baby, he went through a season of not wanting to sleep, so we got no sleep either. If we drove him around in the car, he would go to sleep just fine every time. Finally, we discovered that if we set his car seat on the clothes dryer, the noise, vibration, and low heat would put him to sleep!

The devil, likewise, is persistent in finding a way to accomplish his purpose of distracting us from doing what God is calling us to do. If he can't get you distracted by attacking one area, such as lust or jealousy, he'll move over to another area, such as finances or health. Satan keeps trying until he finds what works. He is not after your car or your money, he is after *you*. He must find an avenue. Hell doesn't need washers and dryers or backed-up sinks. He is just looking for a way to get you off-focus, lull you to sleep, and then do some real damage.

The enemy will be persistent in trying to distract you.
Stay alert and don't give up.

This reminds me of when we used to set traps. The bait was there to camouflage the trap—to keep it from being seen. That's what the devil does. You don't see his trap because you are looking at the bait.

If you watch a movie about any of the military's special forces, you see how carefully they walk to avoid traps. They have been trained to see things that other people miss. They don't step where other people would step because their senses are fine-tuned. They put more of an investment in their training than the average soldier.

Many people want the "Green Beret" status without the investment of the time it takes to get to that place. It just doesn't work that way, though. You can't just get a sheet of paper saying that you are a Green Beret without going through the process. If you skipped the process, you wouldn't really be able to walk in that calling successfully.

Don't try to skip the process – you'll miss the lessons.

In Matthew 25, verses 1-13, we can read the story of the ten virgins who were waiting for the bridegroom. Five were prepared with their lamps and extra oil and five were not. None of them knew when the bridegroom was coming, but that was no excuse not to be prepared. The bridegroom was delayed in arriving, and so the virgins fell asleep.

When the bridegroom came, the girls awoke and prepared their lamps. The lamps of the five foolish virgins were going out because they didn't have enough oil in their lamps. They began to beg of the others to give them some of their oil. The wise ones refused, explaining that there would not be enough for *them* if they agreed.

The wise virgins were not rebuked for not sharing because the foolish virgins could have bought oil for themselves, but they chose not to. Laziness had won out. They waited until the last minute and then tried to put a guilt trip on the ones who had been prepared. Those who were ready went with him to the wedding and the door was shut. Afterward, the foolish virgins came begging for the bridegroom to open the door to them and he said, ". . . I do not know you" (Matthew 25:12, NKJV).

We must stay vigilant, do all we are asked to do, and stay prepared. We may have some turbulence in our economy, but we should not be afraid to go out and buy what we need or make deals when He tells us to. You must be assured of what He is commanding you to do. If He tells you to go out and buy something now, do it and don't wait. You may think you have time, but the foolish virgins missed the opportunity when the door was opened.

Stay vigilant and stay prepared. Don't hesitate when a command is given.

Malachi 3:10 says, "I am the Lord All-Powerful, and I challenge you to put me to the test. Bring the entire ten percent [the tithe] into the storehouse, so there will be food in my house. Then I will open the windows of heaven and flood you with blessing after blessing" (CEV). I personally believe that the "open windows of heaven" referred to in this verse are windows or doors of opportunity. You must move when God says to move and not be influenced by what the world is saying or even by what your mind may be saying.

If God says to make a move, obey Him. God already has tomorrow figured out. Stay on your wall. Stay about your purpose. If God says to do something, go ahead and get it done. Stay on it and keep at it.

Hold on to your promises and wage warfare with the Word. Remember Whose you are. Fully obey what He has asked you to do and don't quit too soon! Don't compromise, settling for less than what He has promised you. Speak to the mountains in front of you, ignore the distractions and oppositions, resist the enemy, and don't give up! Go after all that He has promised.

Believe God for the spirit of wisdom and revelation to come so that you know His plan for your life and stay with it until you have accomplished all that God intends for you to do. It is time to take back what belongs to us as individuals, families, and the body of Christ. We must surrender to His will and His plan – body, soul, and spirit – and never stop short of what He says to do.

Then, after having done all, we will stand!

About the Author

Bryan and his wife Rhonda are the lead and founding pastors of New Life Church. The church has three campuses serving the areas of Augusta, Georgia and North Augusta, South Carolina. New Life Church reaches within their community and globally to Kenya, Zambia, Aruba, Peru, and Belize. Bryan and Rhonda have been pastoring for 24 years. They have one son, Carter, who is married to Elizabeth Ann.

Thank you for your support of this ministry. It is Bryan's desire to encourage you to develop a deep relationship with the Lord and live victoriously surrendered to Him. If this book has helped you gain a deeper understanding of the value of standing firm in faith, please rate this book on Amazon and share about it with others. Also, please look for Rhonda Matthew's engaging book *The Person of the Holy Spirit*, also available on Amazon in paperback and Kindle formats.

Made in the
USA
Columbia, SC